Sweet and Low: Poems for a Healing Heart

Sarah Marie

BookLeaf Publishing

Sweet and Low: Poems for a Healing Heart
© 2022 Sarah Marie

Presentation by *BookLeaf Publishing*

Web: www.bookleafpub.com

E-mail: info@bookleafpub.com

ISBN: 9789395890922

First edition 2022

DEDICATION

To Abigail,

In thy eternal sleep

Ghosts of Yesterday

I heard some joyous cries
   Of laughter through the air,
It caught me by surprise
   For a presence I felt there.

The subtle giggles lent
   A certain Yuletide cheer...
I'll never know what bent
   The children that were here.

I hear the little echoes
   Of their voices sweet,
And where the wee soul goes
   With candid hastened feet.

Now that I can hear it,
   I wish that I could see
The happy little spirits
   Who present themselves to me.

So many choose to forfeit
   To hear these folks at play...
I'll never once forget
   These ghosts of Yesterday.

Sweet And Low

Sweet and low, sweet and low,
We thought you were asleep;
Thus quietude deceived us so
That in the womb you keep!
Long, long, so long ago
T'was ordained your soul must go;
Rest in peace, my child so sweet,
In thy eternal sleep.

Merry and whole, merry and whole,
The sound of your heartbeat,
We thought it was a sign of hope
That you would live to see;
But we were wrong, as you know,
For your dancing little soul
Is joyous while I sit and weep;
Sleep, my dear child, sleep.

There We Will Be Friends Again

Over the hedge and through the mountains,
Is a place where you and I will go.
Where we can see each other again,
And sing, and dance, be children once more !
There will be no troubles, scorn or trials,
Our hearts will heal and souls amend
Where all are dead, yet everyone lives,
There we will be friends again.

Around the valley and over the river,
Someday we will meet there.
You and I shall come hither,
And again be our childish pair.
Look toward the days to come,
For this is our omen,
When we go after life is done,
There we will be friends again!

Sweet Silence

How soft and serene
Are the splendors unseen?
And the pleasant glow
Of the things unknown,
As the gossiping gales
Whisper sweet tales,
And secretive nymphs
Tell in sweet silence.

How sweet the song
That's merry and long?
They kiss the faces
Of our dear embraces!
The wonderful gift
Of the walloping wisp,
That tells of their presence
In their sweet silence.

Dreamland

In dreamland deep
　The slumberer sleeps
In twilight depths
　Where dreams are kept;
And folly of day
　Is swept away.

Lady Spring

Lady Spring hath come in her finest adornment
To appeal to all those of offering praise;
In her sweet selection of ancient beauties
That gently whispers of lovely Spring days!

Born to us in the crystal dawn of time,
She flourished delights in the wakeful morn,
And tenderly woke the sleeping blossoms
That charm our hearts with their beauty's lore.

Sweetly she sings in the mist of twilight,
When creatures of earth and sky slumber deep,
As she caresses the earth with fine fingers
And with dew of nightfall, she lets it steep.

Her voice that of a robin's, chaste and pure,
Puts to rest the mind of the newborn lamb,
As she lifts it sweetly and carries it home
To the flock in the pasture, and worrisome dam.

She walks through the valleys of rainbow
depths,
And wades in brooks of reflecting secrets;
In her bosom lay the bygone memories
Of each generation in their youthful fits.

Her thoughts are a mystery, unique, divine,
She smiles and murmurs of things unknown;
By which only the clouds can mirror back
For only to them has her face been shown…

In the mystic light of the magical moon,
She dances on rivers and lakes of song:
The notes drift softly through the limpid air
And lulls the distant echoing throng.

As she walks through the meadows of fervent delight,
Every new blossom patiently listens,
For her sweet whisper is placid and calm,
And on every new bud a name is christened.

She hungers for merriment and thirsts for delight
And savors the taste of a lover's romance;
For she knows all too well the yearning heart
And amply the bitter heartbreak of ill-chance…

At the birth of the garden, when all was at peace,
Eden, her lover, in royalty reigned—
But torn from her heart in bitter exile,
She cries many tears till their love is regained.

And in the hours of the last August dusk
She sits in the darkness of autumn tears;

The parting is solemn, yet hope may endure
For when she comes frolicking back next year!

On The Grassy Lea

How I miss the days we'd stand
Close together, hand-in-hand,
Among the purple scented lilies,
Pansies, roses, daffodillies—
Lightly on the slender fern
You'd speak to me most tender,
Voice that of the waving sea
On sacred shores of Galilee.

O come back to me, my love,
Or I shall come join thee above!
No longer shall my foot fall
Along this primitive stone wall,
Nor hear the crickets airy lilt
Come from under grassy tilt,
That charmed the spirits of the lea,
When you had been here with me!

The Song of Spring

Don't you hear the jubilant cry
Echo through the sapphire sky?
The merry piping of the clouds,
Dancing 'long in hefty mounds,
Clear across the gleeful sea
And guides the songbird's melody.
Gliding rays of stilted gold
Through the winter's wimple folds,
On the satin field's grass
Shining like untainted glass.
The genteel breeze's subtle coon
Wakes the baby flower bloom
By setting off the sacred keys
Of the harbored emerald trees.
When all the world does so sing,
Hark! 'Tis the Song of Spring!

By The Sea

Indented by the little prints
Of little childrens' feet,
And dappled by the subtle hints
Where lovers used to meet;

Love and Joy were by the Sea
Consisting perfect rhyme,
Echoing their sweet melody—
Whose notes still faintly chime.

Peace still walks along the shore
Her sweet face turned alee,
Faintly teaching ancient lore
By singing with the Sea.

Una's Love

A secret love, so hidden deep,
That no one could express how steep,
Though I know through beseeming guise
How she adored his bright gray eyes,
And when he spoke, her gentle sighs
Escaped in such a misty esteem—
So full of longing it should seem
That he were of her precious dream.

A love so deep, yet did not show,
That even the boy did not know
How she looked beseechingly
Unto him in passion keen,
And heart danced to his poetry!
How timidly she'd give her praise
To him, in their golden days
Of secret love of mysteries.

Just as he who never knew,
She won't know he loved her, too.
But that time has come to pass;
She must take up the bitter glass
That her love lay 'somewhere in France.'
Forevermore will she miss,
On her rosy cheek— the bliss!
Of his unforgotten kiss!

A Miserable Day

Dark and dingy and gray,
Rain pours from the sky,
A most undesirable way
To start one's morning,
Leaving a misty aray
With nothing but mumbling and moaning.
Oh, what a miserable day!

Arising from the misty dawn,
White, frosty feathers fall,
Glistening in the winter sun,
And gather on the soggy ground.
A crystal winter frost-like fay
Of snow and icy mound.
Oh, what a beautiful day!

Outside, the world transforms
With a covering of snow,
Everyone bundles up warm,
Because it snows intensely!
The world, now happy and gay,
Is enjoyed immensely.
Oh, what a wonderful day!

My Maple Grove

I remembered a place
　　I liked to go...
My father's beautiful
　　Maple Grove.

In my youthful days of
　　Dark autumn eves,
I walked in the hue of
　　Tremulous leaves...

In the serene twilight,
　　When fairies fly;
The woodfolk came near and
　　Waved cares good-bye...

Precious was the freedom
　　Spent on a stroll,
Where stillness of moment
　　Refreshed my soul;

The peacefulness would last
　　Many hours
As I made friends amongst
　　Only flowers…

Bent on a memory,
    Lost to delight...
In the airy walks of
    Maple moonlight!

Seldom do I bother
    To let my mind rove,
Whether I shall see my
    Small maple grove.

Forever and A Day

I saw your philtrum peaked rosebud lips
Breath steadily eternal breath;
Your precious eyes and fingertips,
That touched a life of happiness, not of death,
And for temporal time, you were mine for a
day--
But in the night you stole away...

For only a day I had you in my arms,
Your cheek laying upon my breast,
Where you left your fresh residue
To stain a reminder upon my chest.
And so, happily ever after came
As I watched them take you away?

And so the world would think this true--
But is a disastrous thing to believe in;
For when I die and come to you,
That is when our lives begin!
So in heaven we will stay
Together forever-- plus a day.

A Promise

Out of the secret
Chambers of the heart
Came my sacred vow;
But when you did part
I remembered how
I could not keep it.

My promise still stands
In spite of your death,
For your wee spirit
Knows eternal breath;
So I hold to it
With faltering hands.

At the end of time
I know you'll be there,
Patiently waiting
In knowledge and care.
I'll bring when coming
This promise of mine.

I uttered the words
With light-hearted trust,
And didn't think you
Would turn into dust;

But both of us grew
As two nests of birds.

That caref'ly placed rhyme
Remains unfulfilled,
And shall remain, too,
Till life is unveil'd;
And then I'll show you
This promise of mine.

On My Way To Neverland

On my way to Neverland
I met a decent boy;
His looks were fine and airs were grand
But one this did annoy:
His youthful tongue ceaselessly rung
About when he grows up.
He chattered like a nightingale
About things like business stages,
Taxing, bills and housing sales,
And work for daily wages.

We sat upon the grass of youth
To have our conversation,
While beside the path that leadeth
To my destination;
But still his tongue went steadily on
About how he would develop;
And raising in a manly voice,
And speaking such in earnest,
He told of how great men rejoice
And I began to take interest.

Anon a gloom came to his eyes
And fell oft to look southward-
His shoulders drooped in burdened guise

As bearing something awkward;
Which ceased his tongue, his voice was gone
And all at once he'd grown up.
He'd worked so hard to attain
That glorified atonement,
Which seemed to him life's sustain
But may be lost in a moment!

Oh! I've lost my way to Neverland!
A wretched act of ignorance,
To listen to him on the strand
And give way to his countenance.
His wayward tongue, it's will be done,
And now, I too, must grow up!
The golden days have long since passed,
And blind I gave them freely,
A distant memory they last
And life now lies before me.

Morning Milking

It is always a delightful thing
  To go out in the morning;
To smell the freshness of the air
  And hear my milk goat's bleating.
To sit on the comfy wooden stand,
  Following my goat's command—
Charmed that she turns and licks my arm
  Like a mother and baby's band.

Who Do You Love More?

"Please tell me, Mother,
Who you love more:
Me or my Father?"
Was the child's implore.
The mother smiled,
Though taken aback,
And lifted the child
Onto her lap,
"Alas, my dear child,
You must understand,
That lots of my love
Goes to my husband!
He's such a dear man,
Whom I've love ever since
The day that I met him.
Now, does this make sense?
I didn't know him till later-
About twenty years old-
And when we got together,
My heart was half whole.
But I've loved you since
You were first known.
The first moments of life,
When you were first sewn.
I love not one of you

More than the other,
But my love for you,
Is that of a Mother."

Little Rachel

Squeak off the bed and into the hall,
Pattering feet on the floor,
Dimpled fingers sliding 'cross the wall,
And creaking open the door.

In pops a little redhead of curls,
Smothering giggles with a white paw.
Sneaking past the sleeping girls,
And climbs onto the bed so tall.

Atop she gives a triumphant smile,
Wrinkling her nose and showing her teeth,
And looks at her sister while
Lifting the blanket, she crawls underneath.

Consoled in her place of confinement,
She declares in a pleasant whine
That comes from such an infant,
"It cuddle time."

Bittersweet

A chalice, full of sweet memories,
Bittered by the sorrowful weakness
Of tears that follow the tragedies
Of death. Slowly they fall into its contents
And the liquid, brimming with sweetness,
Distorted. As the shadow darkens
Over the soul and leaves sweet bitterness.
The taste remains yet a conjunction
Of the joy of what once was had,
And sorrow of what has now been lost;
For all the sweetness of memory
Of past remains yet undrunk, as tears
Refill the emptying cup. Ever
Filling, the bittersweet drink settles
Upon the soul, ever eternal.

The Hands That Hold Me

I know I am safer in Your hands than in my own,
For my hands do not bare the scars which they
deserve
Because while in my shackles, You went to trial
alone.

Your hands are holy because a nail pierced
through them
As You hung on the cross, and my life hung on
the line;
But it's the hands that were nailed that now hold
me.

Your side was stabbed with a spear so my soul
would go without wound,
And You were bound in a tomb to free me from
mine
As I follow the trail of dripping blood You left
behind.

My hands were dirty and You washed them with
the blood from your own
As it poured and You paled and as life left Your
eyes;

And a new everlasting life entered the chambers
of mine.

It was through the wine that You earnestly
declined
That I feel no pain when a needle of trouble
pricks my soul,
While Your suffering hands bare a burning hole–

You said it was finished when I was too scared
to begin;
You breathed out your last as I was afraid to
breath in–
You lost Your life because I defied my right to
live.

It was with rusty nails that holy blood was shed,
And my hands bare no scars where they should
be instead–
But I take comfort in the nails of the hands that
hold me.

The Alpine Path

Walking down the Alpine Path
Of golden soil, rich and trend,
In the wych-elms emerald cast
Beneath the fir and elders' bends,
In the glistering light of the moon
Along the grasses' crystalling dew.

Through the elders, shadows creep
Across the mourned bleeding hearts,
Dancing on the violets sweet,
And sheds the dancing firs apart
With it's slender sweeping hand,
Envious of the moon's claimed land.

Sparrows, larks and robins keep
Singing of the olden days,
In the birks' dark, cistern deep
To the moon's unchastened grey,
With the canaries electric shrill
That echoes on this alpine hill.

Through the witching silver mist
The whispering elf-kin fairy guise,
With rosy cheeks and scarlet lips,
Come to watch with keen gray eyes

At me in a most curious whim,
As if I were of immortal kin.

Fervent silver and emerald boughs
Of fairies, blossoms and moons agleam;
Flourished wonders and mystic sounds
Touch upon my cherished dream!
Such a place for fancy's growth
Along the Alpine Path.